THIRD SUNDAY OF JUNE

MY GENIUS FATHER

IMRAN KASHMIRI

Made with ❤ on the Notion Press Platform
www.notionpress.com

Don't be afraid
I'm near to your bed
I will stay here
With you all night long

Don't be afraid
I'm near to your bed
I'll keep your hands in
Mine all night long

A father will always give you the best
A father is present when his little boy
Wants to be helped
In his eyes
A father could give this life
To save his own son

Don't be afraid
I'm near to your bed
I'll sing this song for
You all night long

Contents

Foreword

Don't be afraid
I'm near to your bed
I will stay here
With you all night long
    Don't be afraid
I'm near to your bed
I'll keep your hands in
Mine all night long
      A father will always give you the best
A father is present when his little boy
Wants to be helped
In his eyes
A father could give this life
To save his own son
    Don't be afraid
I'm near to your bed
I'll sing this song for
You all night long

Don't be afraid
I'm near to your bed
I promise i'll be with
You all night long
      A father can feel when his boy is afraid
A father can feel when his fate
Comes to take him away
A father can see what is there in his eyes
A father could give his life
To save his son right now !
    But i have to win
The pain that i feel !
There's nothing to worry about

So let that feeling stand
So let that feeling stand...
    A father can see what is there in his eyes
A father could give his life
To save his son right now

Preface

Anyone can father a child, but being a dad takes a lifetime. Fathers play a role in every child's life that cannot be filled by others. This role can have a large impact on a child and help shape him or her into the person they become.

Acknowledgements

Name:-MOHAMMAD YOUSUF DAR(1975)
FATHER:-ABDUL RAHMAN DAR
MOTHER:-KHATOON (1953)
BROTHERS:-MANZOOR HUSSAIN,ZAFFAR HUSSAIN AND GHULAAM HUSSAIN
SISTERS:- RAFEEKA

Prologue

Fathers, like mothers, are pillars in the development of a child's emotional well-being. Children look to their fathers to lay down the rules and enforce them. They also look to their fathers to provide a feeling of security, both physical and emotional. Children want to make their fathers proud, and an involved father promotes inner growth and strength. Studies have shown that when fathers are affectionate and supportive, it greatly affects a child's cognitive and social development. It also instils over all sense of well-being and self-confidence

Fathers not only influence who we are inside, but how we have relationships with people as we grow. The way a father treats his child will influence what he or she looks for in other people. Friends, lovers, and spouses will all be chosen based on how the child perceived the meaning of the relationship with his or her father. The patterns a father sets in the relationships with his children will dictate how his children relate with other people.

CHAPTER ONE

Father and their sons

Unlike girls, who model their relationships with others based on their father's character, boys model themselves after their father's character. Boys will seek approval from their fathers from a very young age. As human beings, we grow up by imitating the behavior of those around us; that's how we learn to function in the world. If a father is caring and treats people with respect, the young boy will grow up much the same. When a father is absent, young boys look to other male figures to set the "rules" for how to behave and survive in the world.

Father and their Daughters

Young girls depend on their fathers for security and emotional support. A father shows his daughter what a good relationship with a man is like. If a father is loving and gentle, his daughter will look for those qualities in men when she's old enough to begin dating. If a father is strong and valiant, she will relate closely to men of the same character.

Role of a Father (Motivator)

As a dad, you are at times a helper, a coach, and a friend. One of your jobs is to motivate your children toward daily productivity and healthy growth. I find that my kids are not always self-motivated to reach their full potential in character, discipline, and spiritual growth. So when I see that potential, this is where I often find the need to come in, sometimes creatively and other times firmly, to motivate them. Sometimes this is with ideas, incentives, schedules, or simply clear expectations.

Enforcer

Fatherlessness is a great concern in our society today. And one of the greatest disadvantages many kids in fatherless homes face is the lacking male presence and leadership they need. A huge part of having a father in the home is having an enforcer in the home.

Like it or not, kids naturally respond differently to male leadership, especially in the family. Dad being the main enforcer of family rules and boundaries at home also makes a mother's job so much easier.

Encourager

Every child loves positive fatherly encouragement

Because children are born with a desire for their father's approval and attention, one of the best ways to encourage them is to be their biggest cheerleader and their greatest fan. Giving them regular compliments and positive reinforcement in the areas of their strengths can go a long way. I personally have seen the demeanor of my children change when I say encouraging things like, "You're going a great job" or "I'm so glad you're mine." Every child loves positive fatherly encouragement.

Trainer

There are lessons and life skills your child will never learn apart from being taught. Part of the role of fatherhood is training our children to be good at life. From learning how to ride a bike to knowing how to manage good relationships with the opposite sex, and everything in between, your child needs your intentional investment. Yes, it takes time and a bit of inconvenience, but it's so worth it in the long-run.

Counselor

Kids struggle too. Sometimes, as adults, it's easy to forget this because their problems seem so small. Do you remember how small things were big things as a kid? Children don't naturally know how to navigate the issues of life that are thrown at them. That's because they're kids—they're adults in training. They regularly need direction, answers, and advice. Dad, strive to be your children's chief counselor, their go-to for advice. Because they will get it from somewhere, so why not from you?

Parents play very important role in the growth process of their child. In some cases, fathers and mothers complement each other's role but some responsibilities are to be performed solely by the fathers. For the children, father is the hero within the family. The behaviour and activities of a father affect a child immensely so fathers must act responsibly. A responsible father will always ensure that his kids get a healthy environment to grow up physically and mentally both.

Father is Always a Protector

Opens Up the World for the Kids

Unconditional Love

Show Love and Respect for the Partner

Spending Quality Time

Teaching Discipline

Teaching Accountability

Involve In the Studies

Teach Taking Responsibilities

Be a Provider

Father*s Love

It was a long day, but a good one. My family had finished dinner and I was cleaning the dishes. As I washed off the last cup, I felt a gentle tap on my hip. I looked down to see my daughter's innocent brown eyes staring up at me. In her tender voice, she asked, "Daddy, do you love us more when it's our birthday? I mean do you love whoever's birthday it is, more than the other kids on that day?" I knelt down and put my hand on her shoulder. Then I explained to her that my love doesn't change based on birthdays. It doesn't increase nor decrease based on the circumstance. My love is unconditional.

There are so many things a father's love gives and so many things that a lack of it destroys."

There are so many things a father's love gives and so many things that a lack of it destroys. I believe that God gives us the greatest example of a father's love. His love is sacrificial, patient, kind, humble, honest, forgiving, faithful, and selfless. It is constant and unchanging. Those are the things I not only want my life to be about, but I want to make certain my kids know and feel from me. Unfortunately, I am not perfect like God, which includes my fatherhood. I consistently fall short. So I have to ask myself if my kids know their father's love. Here are 5 questions to ask ourselves as dads.

It's right to correct children even though they don't like it. They need boundaries and it's important to be consistently firm in maintaining those boundaries. Disciplining should be done to nurture the heart to a healthy place when it has gone wandering or rebelled. However, anger and a need to control behavior either take over or, at the very least, seep in. Go beyond the behavior and address the motivation. Loving discipline will address the motivators firmly, but calmly. It will also pursue reconciliation and forgiveness in the end.

Watching someone we love go through pain is difficult. It's easy to want them to get over it or toughen up because entering into it with them is painful and awkward. Empathy is hard, but it is a loving response to someone in pain because we are identifying with them. We connect with their pain and communicate that they are not alone. We are there to walk with them and never leave them.

We can't be focused on our kids all of the time and shouldn't be. But do they know that the time spent away is to benefit them? Do they know what we are working on and why we are away? Do they know how we feel about being away from them and perhaps working long hours? There are adult responsibilities we need to attend to. We need to focus on our jobs because our family needs things. They need food, shelter, clothing, etc. Much of the time spent away from them is spent providing these essentials. It's also good for them to know that they are wonderful and important but not the center of the world. I want my kids to know that my focus has a loving purpose even when it isn't on them, but while I'm away, I miss them.

There is so much about the world that doesn't make sense to a child. Childhood is a confusing period all the way through the teen years and even beyond. Sometimes we expect our kids to know things at their young age that we didn't learn until much later. It takes a long time before kids have any kind of understanding of who they really are. It's important to show patience and understanding. In the midst of insecurity and confusion, our love provides gravity.

Father*s Day 2023

sayings about fatherhood. Whether it's your dad, uncle, brother, grandpa — anyone who has been a father figure to you — you want to make sure you express your love and gratitude for him on that third Sunday in June. A personalized card with a special message for dad will let him know how much you appreciate all of his priceless advice and unconditional support.